Pebble® Plus

PIRATES AHOY!

Pirate Ships

by Rosalyn Tucker

Consulting editor: Gail Saunders-Smith, PhD

raintree
a Capstone company — publishers for children

Raintree is an imprint of Capstone Global Library Limited, a company incorporated in England and Wales having its registered office at 7 Pilgrim Street, London, EC4V 6LB – Registered company number: 6695582

www.raintree.co.uk
myorders@raintree.co.uk

Text © Capstone Global Library Limited 2015
The moral rights of the proprietor have been asserted.

Editorial Credits
Michelle Hasselius, editor; Kazuko Collins, designer; Pam Mitsakos, media researcher; Gene Bentdahl, production specialist

ISBN 978 1 406 29352 4
19 18 17 16 15
10 9 8 7 6 5 4 3 2 1

British Library Cataloguing in Publication Data
A full catalogue record for this book is available from the British Library.

Photo Credits
Alamy: © ClassicStock, 9, © PARIS PIERCE, 13; Bridgeman Images: Peter Newark Historical Pictures, 5; Dreamstime: © Gordan, 17; Mary Evans Picture Library, 11; Newscom: ZUMA Press/Jon Mitchell, 21; Shutterstock: Denis Tabler, 15, Elenarts, cover; Superstock, 7, 19
Design Elements: Shutterstock: A-R-T (old paper), La Gorda (rope illustration), vovan (old wood)

Every effort has been made to contact copyright holders of material reproduced in this book. Any omissions will be rectified in subsequent printings if notice is given to the publisher.

All the internet addresses (URLs) given in this book were valid at the time of going to press. However, due to the dynamic nature of the internet, some addresses may have changed, or sites may have changed or ceased to exist since publication. While the author and publisher regret any inconvenience this may cause readers, no responsibility for any such changes can be accepted by either the author or the publisher.

Printed in China by Nordica.
0914/CA21401504

Contents

Sailing the seas

Mighty wooden ships explored the seas
during the Golden Age of Piracy (1690–1730).
Pirates worked hard to look after
their ships. They always had
to be ready for the next raid.

Many sailors feared pirate attacks at sea.

Pirates often stole ships.
But pirate ships needed to
be fast. So pirates made the
ships lighter. The lighter
the ship, the faster it sailed.

After winning a battle, pirates often stole the ship and the treasures on board.

Ship sizes

Small, fast ships made good pirate ships. These ships could easily sneak up on others and attack. Small ships could also hide in shallow waters.

Many pirates
sailed on small ships
called schooners.

A few pirates sailed on large, heavy warships. The warships could not move or turn as quickly as small ships. But large ships could carry more weapons and treasures.

Black Bart sailed one of the largest pirate ships. It had 52 guns on board.

Parts of a ship

A ship's floor is called the deck.

Pirates worked on the deck.

They pulled ropes to move the

sails. Sails filled with wind and

pushed the ship through water.

Every pirate had a job on the ship. Some cleaned the deck or moved the sails.

Pirates stored weapons and food in a room called the hold. Sometimes pirates made secret rooms in the hold to hide treasures.

Treasures such as gold and jewels were hidden in the hold.

Ships in battle

Pirate ships looked scary.

Cannons lined the deck.

Pirate flags with painted bones

and skulls flapped in the wind.

cannons on
a ship

Battles could damage pirate ships. A damaged ship had to be mended quickly. Pirates risked being captured if their ships could not sail.

Pirates had to cover holes made by
cannonballs and mend broken masts on ships.

Pirate ships today

The Golden Age of Piracy is over. Today's pirates do not travel on ships with big sails and heavy cannons. But they still use small, fast boats to attack ships at sea.

modern pirates from Somalia, Africa

Glossary

attack try to hurt someone or something

cannon heavy gun that fires large metal balls

capture take a person or place by force

damage harm done to something

Golden Age of Piracy period from 1690 to 1730, when thousands of people became pirates around the world

pirate person who steals from towns and ships

raid sudden, surprise attack

shallow not deep

treasure gold, jewels, money and other items of value

warship ship with many weapons, made for fighting wars at sea

Books

On a Pirate Ship, Anna Milbourne and Benji Davies
(Usborne Publishing, 2011)

Pirate Ships (See Inside), Rob Lloyd Jones
(Usborne Publishing, 2007).

Pirates (Legends of the Sea), Rebecca Rissman
(Raintree, 2011)

Websites

www.bbc.co.uk/cbeebies/swashbuckle-online/games
Find the treasure and make the pirates walk the plank!
Try these fun pirate games.

www.jerseyheritage.org/learning/teacher-resources-pirates
Do you know the difference between the mast and
the crow's nest? Follow the links to colour and label
a pirate ship, and make your own treasure map!

Index